What is an Election?

By Caryn Jenner

Let's vote!

US Senior Editor Shannon Beatty
US Editor Margaret Parrish
Senior Editor Carrie Love
Project Editor Kritika Gupta
Assistant Editor Gunjan Mewati
Project Art Editors Polly Appleton, Roohi Rais
Assistant Art Editor Bhagyashree Nayak
Jacket Co-ordinator Issy Walsh
Senior Jacket Designer Dheeraj Arora
DTP Designers Sachin Gupta, Nand Kishor Acharya
Picture Researcher Rituraj Singh
Senior Production Editor Jennifer Murray
Production Controller Basia Ossowska
Managing Editors Penny Smith, Monica Saigal
Managing Art Editors Mabel Chan, Ivy Sengupta
Delhi Team Head Malavika Talukder
Publishing Manager Francesca Young
Publishing Director Sarah Larter

Reading Consultant Dr. Barbara Marinak
Subject Consultant Julius Sen

First American Edition, 2020
Published in the United States by DK Publishing
1450 Broadway, Suite 801, New York, New York 10018

DK books are available at special discounts when purchased in bulk for sales promotions,
premiums, fund-raising, or educational use. For details, contact: DK Publishing Special Markets,
1450 Broadway, Suite 801, New York, New York 10018
SpecialSales@dk.com

Printed and bound in China

The publisher would like to thank the following for their kind permission to reproduce their photographs:
(Key: a-above; b-below/bottom; c-center; f-far; l-left; r-right; t-top)
1 iStockphoto.com: E+ / SDI Productions (b). **1–48 Dreamstime.com:** Macrovector (hand icons). **5 iStockphoto.com:** Photodisc /
Image Source. **6-7 Alamy Stock Photo:** 506 collection. **8-9 Alamy Stock Photo:** dpa picture alliance. **10–11 Alamy Stock Photo:**
Gordon M. Grant. **12 Alamy Stock Photo:** Classic Image (c). **13 Alamy Stock Photo:** Ian Dagnall (cb); Lebrecht Music & Arts (tr).
14–15 Alamy Stock Photo: Philip Game. **16 123RF.com:** rawpixel (t). **17 Alamy Stock Photo:** Joseph Gaul (b). **Dreamstime.com:**
Amanda Lewis (c). **18 Getty Images:** DigitalVision / Hill Street Studios (b). **19 Dreamstime.com:** Smandy (t). **20 Alamy Stock Photo:**
Phil Wills. **21 Dreamstime.com:** Georgesheldon (b). **22–23 Alamy Stock Photo:** World Image Archive. **24–25 Alamy Stock Photo:**
dpa picture alliance. **26 Alamy Stock Photo:** Cliff Hide Local News (cb). **27 Alamy Stock Photo:** Mark Kerrison (t). **28 Alamy Stock
Photo:** Colin young-wolff (t). **Dreamstime.com:** Robot100 (cl). **29 Alamy Stock Photo:** ZUMA Press Inc (cla). **Dreamstime.com:**
Robot100 (crb). **30–31 Dreamstime.com:** Mistervlad. **31 Alamy Stock Photo:** robertharding / Adam Woolfitt (t). **32 Alamy Stock
Photo:** IanDagnall Computing (b). **33 Alamy Stock Photo:** Ian Dagnall. **35 Dreamstime.com:** Ekaterina Brazhnikova (crb). **38–39
Getty Images:** The Image Bank / Dirk Anschutz. **40–41 Alamy Stock Photo:** © Bill Bachmann. **42 iStockphoto.com:** Photodisc /
Image Source **Endpaper images:** *Front:* **Alamy Stock Photo:** Hero Images Inc. ; *Back:* **Alamy Stock Photo:** Hero Images Inc.
Cover images: *Front and Back:* **Dreamstime.com:** Macrovector
All other images © Dorling Kindersley
For further information see: www.dkimages.com

For the curious

www.dk.com

Contents

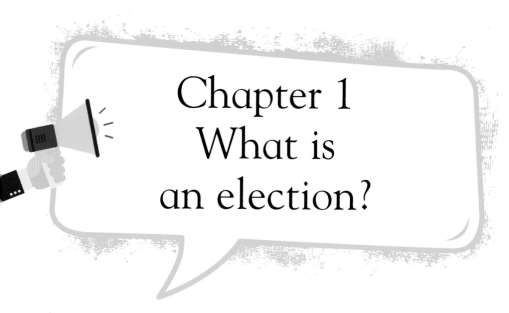

Chapter 1
What is an election?

An election is when a group of people vote for someone to represent them or do something for them. Voting means choosing the person you want. The person with the most votes is the winner.

You might have an election to choose a class president or a team captain.

Students during school elections

Elections are often held to choose the people in government. A government makes the laws for a country or local area.

Former US president Barack Obama meets with members of Congress in 2012.

For example, Americans vote to elect people to Congress and to elect the president of the United States. The people who are elected must promise to do what is best for the country.

People who run for election are called candidates. Each candidate wants voters to think that they are the best person for the job.

Candidates hope that lots of people will vote for them. They travel around and speak to as many voters as they can. This is called a campaign.

Veena George talks to voters in India about what she will do for people if she wins.

The candidates tell voters what they will do if they are elected. Voters use this information to decide who to vote for. Which candidate will do what is best for the country? The voters choose.

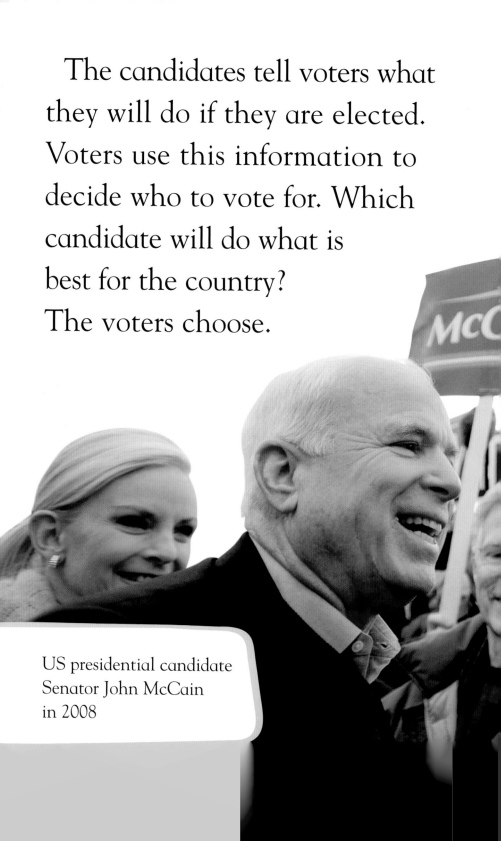

US presidential candidate Senator John McCain in 2008

Election history

The idea of voting a person or a group into power has been around for a long time.

Ancient Greece
The idea of elections comes from ancient Greece. Elections in the city of Sparta were decided by who could shout the loudest.

Europe

Before the 1600s, mainly upper-class men voted in elections in Europe. Many people had to fight for their right to vote.

United States

The United States Constitution was written in 1787. It set out the first rules for the American government and its elections.

Chapter 2
Voting

Who can vote in an election? Voters usually live in the place where the election is held. In most countries, voters also have to be at least 18 years old.

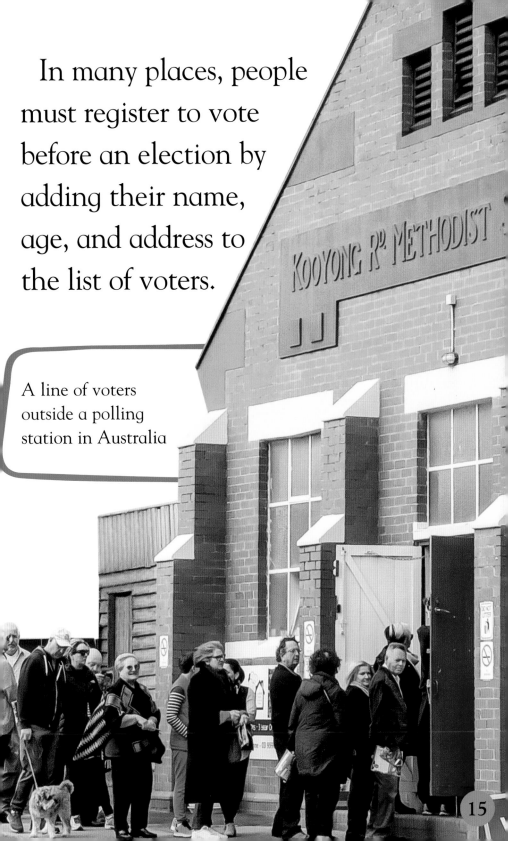

In many places, people must register to vote before an election by adding their name, age, and address to the list of voters.

A line of voters outside a polling station in Australia

KOOYONG Rᵈ METHODIST

In some countries voters must register before voting.

Each voter can vote only once. Most voters go to a special polling station to vote in government elections. Who you vote for is secret. No one should tell you which candidate to choose.

Some people use their computer to vote online. Others send their vote through the mail.

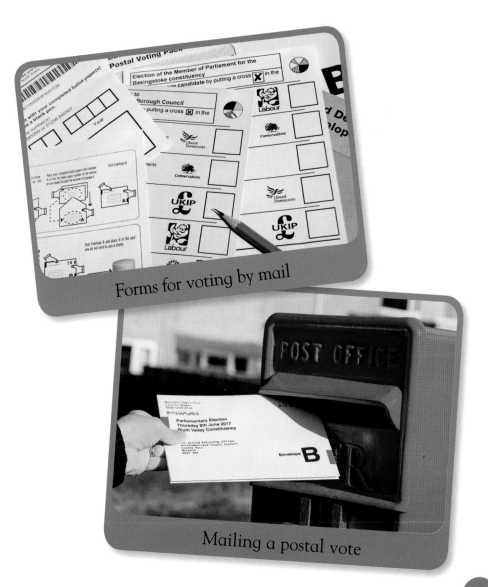

Forms for voting by mail

Mailing a postal vote

At a polling station, voters
cast their ballots in a private booth.
Some polling stations have voting
machines that count the votes for
each candidate.

People voting at a polling
station in the US

A woman puts her ballot in the ballot
box at a polling station in Zambia.

Others list the candidates on
a paper ballot. Each voter picks
the name of their chosen candidate.

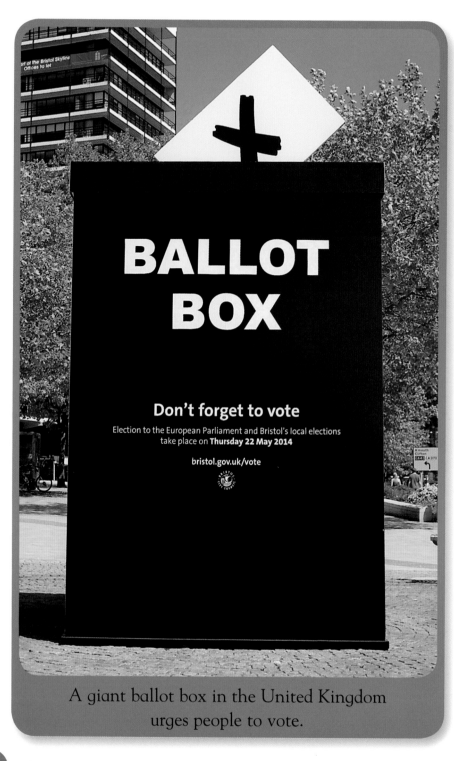

A giant ballot box in the United Kingdom
urges people to vote.

It is very important to vote in elections. No one knows which candidate will win the election, but every vote counts. People who don't vote lose the chance to have their say in how the government is run.

A sign reminds people in the US to use their voting power.

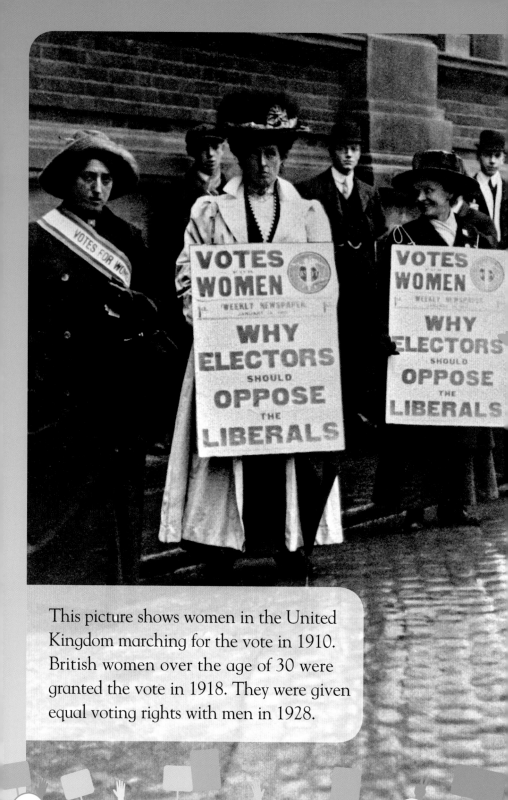

This picture shows women in the United Kingdom marching for the vote in 1910. British women over the age of 30 were granted the vote in 1918. They were given equal voting rights with men in 1928.

The right to vote

All adults should have the right to vote, but in many places some people have not always been allowed to vote. These include women, poor people, and people who belong to a minority religion or race.

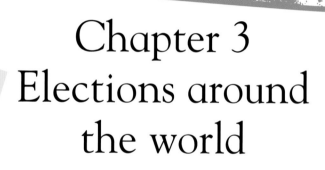

Chapter 3
Elections around the world

A government elected
by the people of a country
is called a democracy.
A democracy gives power to
voters to elect the government.

Members of the Liberal Democratic
Party in Tokyo, Japan, in 2018

In return, the government must do what is best for the people. If they don't, they will lose votes in the next election.

In most countries, candidates belong to a political party. This is a group of people with similar ideas on how to run the country.

The Conservative Party campaigns in the United Kingdom.

The Green Party in the United Kingdom has ideas on how to help save the environment.

A political party campaigns by holding up posters, handing out leaflets, and giving interviews.

Democratic National
Convention in 2008

Symbol of the
Democratic Party

The main political parties in the
United States are the Democrats and
the Republicans. They each have
their own election, called a primary.

In the primary, they choose their party's candidate for president. The Democrats and the Republicans then compete against each other to get their candidate elected.

Republican US presidential candidate Mitt Romney in 2012

Symbol of the Republican Party

Some countries are governed by a group of representatives who meet in a parliament. Voters elect a Member of Parliament (MP) for their local area. The leader of the party with the most MPs becomes leader of the whole country. This leader is called the prime minister.

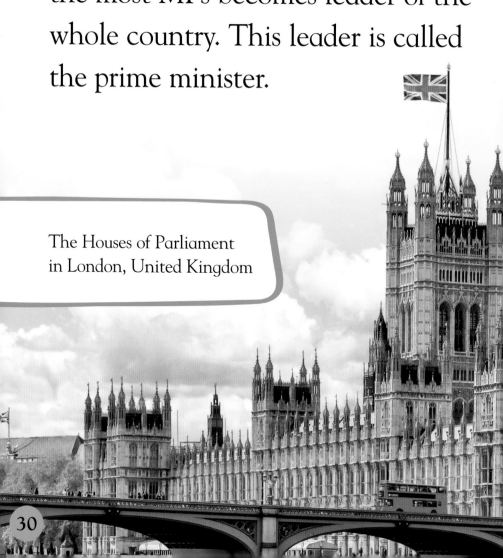

The Houses of Parliament in London, United Kingdom

Inside view of the House of Commons in London, United Kingdom

Not all countries have elections. In some parts of the world people do not have a chance to vote. One person holds the power and makes all of the decisions for everyone.

Emperor Nero reigned as leader of the Roman Empire from 54 CE to 68 CE.

King Louis XIV ruled France
from 1643 to 1715.

Election facts

Here are some fun facts about elections.

Many countries hold elections on a weekend so people have more time to vote.

In Australia, all citizens over the age of 18 are required by law to vote.

In India, there are so many voters that elections can take several weeks.

American astronauts aboard the International Space Station can vote from space.

Chapter 4
Let's elect!

You could hold an election for class president or for student council member. The voters are all the people in your class. Choose a date for the election. Then find out who wants to be a candidate.

Sign up to be a candidate!

The job of the class president or student council member is to make your school a better place.
You would need to:

- ☑ Be friendly with everyone in the class.

- ☑ Listen to ideas from others.

- ☑ Have lots of your own ideas, too.

- ☑ Work with your teachers.

Candidates make posters asking the class to vote for them. They give speeches to the class, too.

A pupil giving a speech at a school election

Candidates tell voters why they would be a good class president or student council member. What would they do for the class or school?

Pass out paper ballots to your class on the day of the election. Ballots should list all of the candidates.

Children vote at a school election.

VOTERS
Get your
ballots here.

Remember, everyone has just one vote. Each voter secretly marks an "X" by the name of their favorite candidate. They then put their paper ballot into a ballot box.

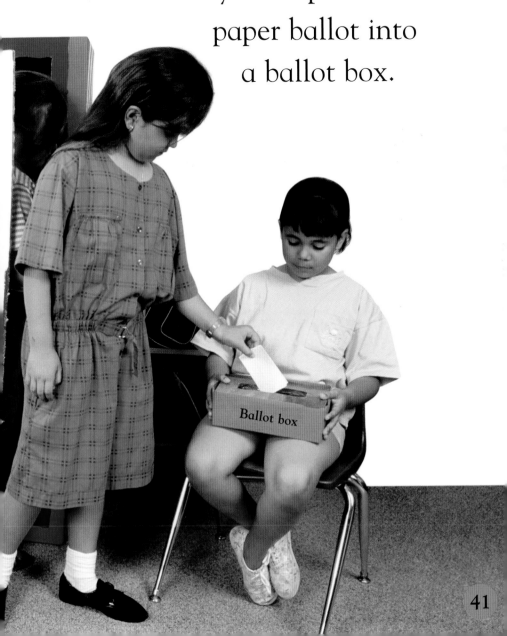

Carefully count the votes. The person with the most votes wins the election. Congratulations!

Winning the election is just the first step. The voters think that the new class president or student council member will do a good job for the class. That's why they won the election. Now it's time for them to get to work!

Counting the votes for class president

Quiz

1 What is a government elected by the people of a country called?

2 What is someone competing in an election called?

3 How old do voters need to be in most countries to vote?

4 How many times can a voter vote in an election?

5 Where do most voters go to vote?

6 Which country did the idea of elections come from?

7 When was the United States Constitution written?

 8 What are the two main political parties in the United States called?

 9 When did women in the United Kingdom first get to vote in an election?

Answers to the quiz:

1. Democracy; 2. Candidate; 3. 18 years old; 4. Once; 5. A polling station; 6. Ancient Greece; 7. 1787; 8. Democrats and Republicans; 9. 1918.

Glossary

ballot
An official list of candidates in an election.

convention
A large meeting of a political party.

democracy
A government chosen by the people.

government
Representatives of the people who make the laws in a country.

parliament
A type of elected government.

president
A name for the leader of a country.

prime minister
The leader of a country and of a parliament.

Index

A LEVEL FOR EVERY READER

This book is a part of an exciting four-level reading series to support children in developing the habit of reading widely for both pleasure and information. Each book is designed to develop a child's reading skills, fluency, grammar awareness, and comprehension in order to build confidence and enjoyment when reading.

Ready for a Level 2 (Beginning to Read) book

A child should:

- be able to recognize a bank of common words quickly and be able to blend sounds together to make some words.
- be familiar with using beginner letter sounds and context clues to figure out unfamiliar words.
- sometimes correct their reading if it doesn't look right or make sense.
- be aware of the need for a slight pause at commas and a longer one at periods.

A valuable and shared reading experience

For many children, reading requires much effort, but adult participation can make reading both fun and easier. Here are a few tips on how to use this book with a young reader:

Check out the contents together:
- read about the book on the back cover and talk about the contents page to help heighten interest and expectation.
- discuss new or difficult words.
- talk about labels, annotations, and pictures.

Support the reader:
- tell the child the title and help them predict what the book will be about.
- give the book to the young reader to turn the pages.
- where necessary, encourage longer words to be broken into syllables, sound out each one, and then flow the syllables together; ask the child to reread the sentence to check the meaning.
- encourage the reader to vary their voice as they read; demonstrate how to do this, if helpful.

Talk at the end of each page:
- ask questions about the text and the meaning of some of the words used—this helps develop comprehension skills.
- read the quiz at the end of the book and encourage the reader to answer the questions, if necessary, by turning back to the relevant pages to find the answers.

Reading consultant: Dr. Barbara Marinak, Dean and Professor of Education at Mount St. Mary's University, Maryland.